NOT THAT HE BROUGHT FLOWERS

Not That He Brought Flowers

★

R. S. THOMAS

RUPERT HART-DAVIS
LONDON
1968

© *R. S. Thomas* 1968
First Published 1968
Rupert Hart-Davis Ltd

3 Upper James Street
Golden Square
London W1

Printed in Great Britain by
Cox & Wyman Ltd
London, Reading and Fakenham

SBN: 246.98580.1

CONTENTS

CAREERS

Fifty-two years,
most of them taken in
growing or in the
illusion of it—what does the mem-
ory number as one's
property? The broken elbow?
the lost toy? The pain has
vanished, but the soft flesh
that suffered it is mine still.

There is a house with
a face mooning at the glass
of windows. Those eyes—I look
at not with them, but something of
their melancholy I
begin to lay claim to as my own.

A boy in school:
his lessons are
my lessons, his
punishments I learn to deserve.
I stand up in him,
tall as I am
now, but without per-
spective. Distant objects
are too distant, yet will arrive
soon. How his words
muddle me; how my deeds
betray him. That is not
our intention; but where I should

be one with him, I am one now
with another. Before I had time
to complete myself, I let her share
in the building. This that I am
now—too many
labourers. What is mine is
not mine only: her love, her
child wait for my slow
signature. Son, from the mirror
you hold to me I turn
to recriminate. That likeness
you are at work upon—it hurts.

A GRAVE UNVISITED

There are places where I have not been;
Deliberately not, like Søren's grave
In Copenhagen. Seeing the streets
With their tedious reproduction
Of all streets, I preferred Dragort,
The cobbled village with its flowers
And pantiles by the clear edge
Of the Baltic, that extinct sea.

What they could do to anchor him
With the heaviness of a nation's
Respectability they have done,
I am sure. I imagine the size
Of his tombstone, the solid marble
Cracking his bones; but would he have been
There to receive this toiling body's
Pilgrimage a few months back,
Had I made it?
          What is it drives a people
To the rejection of a great
Spirit, and after to think it returns
Reconciled to the shroud
Prepared for it? It is Luke's gospel
Warns us of the danger
Of scavenging among the dead
For the living—so I go
Up and down with him in his books,
Hand and hand like a child
With its father, pausing to stare
As he did once at the mind's country.

NO

And one said, This man can sing;
Let's listen to him. But the other,
Dirt on his mind, said, No, let's
Queer him. And the first, being weak,
Consented. So the Thing came
Nearer him, and its breath caused
Him to retch, and none knew why.
But he rested for one long month,
And after began to sing
For gladness, and the Thing stood,
Letting him, for a year, for two;
Then put out its raw hand
And touched him, and the wound took
Over, and the nurses wiped off
The poetry from his cracked lips.

THE OBSERVER

Catrin lives in a nice place
Of bracken, a looking-glass
For the sea that not far off
Glitters. 'You live in a nice place,
Catrin'. The eyes regard me
Unmoved; the wind fidgets
With her hair. Her tongue is a wren
Fluttering in the mouth's cage.

Here is one whom life made,
Omitting an ingredient,
For fun; for luck? How should I know
Its motives, who was not born
To question them, only to see
What I see: the golden landscape
Of nature, with the twisted creatures
Crossing it, each with his load.

ST JULIAN AND THE LEPER

Though all ran from him, he did not
Run, but awaited
Him with his arms
Out, his ears stopped
To his bell, his alarmed
Crying. He lay down
With him there, sharing his sores'
Stench, the quarantine
Of his soul; contaminating
Himself with a kiss,
With the love that
Our science has disinfected.

WEDLOCK

He is out late at night
In the landrover. I hear him going home
In the cold hours; he is up before me
At raw tasks. Out in his hard cab
Of noise he invests the morning
With purpose. I infer a vast
Idleness in the way I spread
Some volume not to be made
Productive like the acres he turns
Mechanically.
              Would I exchange
My life? I know that kitchen,
The values that were asserted
Through long years, through centuries.
The power that has been laid on
Of late cannot conceal
The emptiness. Seated at table
At his brief meal, he rests both his arms
On the oilcloth and looks down,
Unseeing. His ear takes in
Old questions, to which he must nod
Affirmatives. And the land waits.
And the beasts wait for him to finish
His hunked food. And in the village
A girl stares at her lined face
In the looking glass and speaks his name
Joylessly, and the man speaks it
To the mother and their hands tighten
Their grip on this that you call life.

CONCESSION

Not that he brought flowers
Except for the eyes' blue,
Perishable ones, or that his hands,
Famed for kindness were put then
To such usage; but rather that, going
Through flowers later, she yet could feel
These he spared perhaps for my sake.

SIR GELLI MEURIG
(Elizabethan)

I imagine it, a land
Rain-soaked, far away
In the west, in time;
The sea folded too rough
On the shingle, with hard
Breakers and steep
To climb; but game-ridden
And lining his small table
Too thickly—Gelli Meurig,
Squire of a few
Acres, but swollen-headed
With dreaming of a return
To incense, to the confections
Of worship; a Welsh fly
Caught in a web spun
For a hornet.
            Don't blame him.
Others have turned their backs,
As he did, and do so still,
On our land. Leaves light
The autumn, but not for them.
Emptily the sea's cradle
Rocks. They want the town
And its baubles; the fine clothes
They dress one in, who manage
The strings. Helplessly they dance
To a mad tune, who at home
In the bracken could have remained
Humble but free.

CHRISTMAS

There is a morning;
Time brings it nearer,
Brittle with frost
And starlight. The owls sing
In the parishes. The people rise
And walk to the churches'
Stone lanterns, there to kneel
And eat the new bread
Of love, washing it down
With the sharp taste
Of blood they will shed.

THE GREEN ISLE

It is the sort of country that,
After leaving, one is ashamed of
Being rude about. That gentleness
Of green nature, reflected
In its people—what has one done
To deserve it? They sit about
Over slow glasses, discussing,
Not the weather, the news,
Their families, but the half
Legendary heroes of old days:
Women who gave their name
To a hill, who wore the stars
For bracelet; clanking warriors,
Shearing the waves with their swords.

That man shuffling dustily,
His pants through, to the door
Of the gin shop, is not as mean
As he looks; he has the tongue
For which ale is but the excuse
To trespass in golden meadows
Of talk, poaching his words
From the rich, but feasting on them
In that stale parlour with the zest
And freedom of a great poet.

SHRINE AT CAPE CLEAR

She is more white than the sea's
Purest spray, and colder
To touch. She is nourished
By salt winds, and the prayers
Of the drowned break on her. She smiles
At the stone angels, who have turned
From the sea's truth to worship
The mystery of her dumb child.

The bay brings her the tribute
Of its silences. The ocean has left
An offering of the small flowers
Of its springs; but the men read,
Beyond the harbour on the horizon,
The fury of its obituaries.

THE FISHERMAN

A simple man,
He liked the crease on the water
His cast made, but had no pity
For the broken backbone
Of water or fish.

One of his pleasures, thirsty,
Was to ask a drink
At the hot farms;
Leaving with a casual thank you,
As though they owed it him.

I could have told of the living water
That springs pure.
He would have smiled then,
Dancing his speckled fly in the shallows,
Not understanding.

TRAETH MAELGWN

Blue sea; clouds coming up
For convention only; the marks
On the sand, that mean nothing
And don't have to to the fat,
Monoglot stranger. Maelgwn
Was here once, juggling
With the sea; there were rulers
In Wales then, men jealous
Of her honour. He put down
Rivals, made himself king
Of the waves, too; his throne
Buoyant—that rocking beacon
Its image. He kept his power
By intelligence; we lose
Ours for lack of it,
Holding our caps out
Beside a framed view
We never painted, counting
The few casual cowries
With which we are fobbed off.

LLANRHAEADR YM MOCHNANT

This is where he sought God.
And found him? The centuries
Have been content to follow
Down passages of serene prose.

There is no portrait of him
But in the gallery of
The imagination: a brow
With the hair's feathers
Spilled on it? a cheek
Too hollow? rows of teeth
Broken on the unmanageable bone

Of language? In this small room
By the river expiating the sin
Of his namesake?
                          The smooth words
Over which his mind flowed
Have become an heirloom. Beauty
Is how you say it, and the truth,
Like this mountain-born torrent,
Is content to hurry
Not too furiously by.

AFTER THE LECTURE

I am asking the difficult question. I need help.
I'm not asking from ill will.
I have no desire to see you coping
Or not coping with the unmanageable coils
Of a problem frivolously called up.
I've read your books, had glimpses of a climate
That is rigorous, though not too hard
For the spirit. I may have grown
Since reading them; there is no scale
To judge by, neither is the soul
Measurable. I know all the tropes
Of religion, how God is not there
To go to; how time is what we buy
With his absence, and how we look
Through the near end of the binocular at pain,
Evil, deformity. I have tried
Bandaging my sharp eyes
With humility, but still the hearing
Of the ear holds; from as far off as Tibet
The cries come.
                        From one not to be penned
In a concept, and differing in kind
From the human; whose attributes are the negations
Of thought; who holds us at bay with
His symbols, the opposed emblems
Of hawk and dove, what can my prayers win
For the kindred, souls brought to the bone
To be tortured, and burning, burning
Through history with their own strange light?

RESORT

The sea flicks its spray over it.
Occasionally a high tide
Swills its cellars. For the rest
There are only the few streets
With the boredom of their windows.
People, people: the erect species
With its restlessness and the need to pay—
What have they come here to find?
Must they return to the vomit
Of the factories? On the conveyor belt
Of their interests they circle the town
To emerge jaded at the pier;
To look at the water with dull eyes
Resentfully, not understanding
A syllable. Did they expect
The sea, too, to be bi-lingual?

SAILORS' HOSPITAL

It was warm
Inside, but there was
Pain there. I came out
Into the cold wind
Of April. There were birds
In the brambles' old,
Jagged iron, with one striking
Its small song. To the west,
Rising from the grey
Water, leaning one
On another were the town's
Houses. Who first began
That refuse: time's waste
Growing at the edge
Of the clean sea? Some sailor,
Fetching up on the
Shingle before wind
Or current, made it his
Harbour, hung up his clothes
In the sunlight; found women
To breed from—those sick men
His descendants. Every day
Regularly the tide
Visits them with its salt
Comfort; their wounds are shrill
In the rigging of the
Tall ships.

          With clenched thoughts,
That not even the sky's
Daffodil could persuade

To open, I turned back
To the nurses in their tugging
At him, as he drifted
Away on the current
Of his breath, further and further,
Out of hail of our love.

RESERVOIRS

There are places in Wales I don't go:
Reservoirs that are the subconscious
Of a people, troubled far down
With gravestones, chapels, villages even;
The serenity of their expression
Revolts me, it is a pose
For strangers, a watercolour's appeal
To the mass, instead of the poem's
Harsher conditions. There are the hills,
Too; gardens gone under the scum
Of the forests; and the smashed faces
Of the farms with the stone trickle
Of their tears down the hills' side.

Where can I go, then, from the smell
Of decay, from the putrefying of a dead
Nation? I have walked the shore
For an hour and seen the English
Scavenging among the remains
Of our culture, covering the sand
Like the tide and, with the roughness
Of the tide, elbowing our language
Into the grave that we have dug for it.

COMMUTERS

They get up; they catch buses.
They are cold, unexcited.
They leave irritable mothers
For employers of the same
Irritableness. Their progress
Is from uncouth fields to
Uncouth houses. They leave
The peasantry to its labour,
Me to mine. They return
With the dusk. We watch them,
I from my small room,
The farmers from the cinders
Of a day that has gone out.
We are young to teach.
They are old to learn.
Between us we put down
The plain, bald facts of our life,
A recipe for our children.

TOUCHING

She kept touching me,
As a woman will
Accidentally, so the response,
When given, is
A presumption.
                 I retained my
Balance, letting her sway
To her cost. The lips' prose
Ticked on, regulating
Her voltage.
                   Such insulation!
But necessary; their flair
For some small fun with
The current being
An injustice.
It is the man burns.

THE PRIEST

The priest picks his way
Through the parish. Eyes watch him
From windows, from the farms;
Hearts wanting him to come near.
The flesh rejects him.

Women, pouring from the black kettle,
Stir up the whirling tea-grounds
Of their thoughts; offer him a dark
Filling in their smiling sandwich.

Priests have a long way to go.
The people wait for them to come
To them over the broken glass
Of their vows, making them pay
With their sweat's coinage for their correction.

He goes up a green lane
Through growing birches; lambs cushion
His vision. He comes slowly down
In the dark, feeling the cross warp
In his hands; hanging on it his thought's icicles.

'Crippled soul', do you say? looking at him
From the mind's height; 'limping through life
On his prayers. There are other people
In the world, sitting at table
Contented, though the broken body
And the shed blood are not on the menu'.

'Let it be so', I say. 'Amen and amen'.

WELCOME TO WALES

Come to Wales
To be buried; the undertaker
Will arrange it for you. We have
The sites and a long line
Of clients going back
To the first milkman who watered
His honour. How they endow
Our country with their polished
Memorials! No one lives
In our villages, but they dream
Of returning from the rigours
Of the pound's climate. Why not
Try it? We can always raise
Some mourners, and the amens
Are ready. This is what
Chapels are for; their varnish
Wears well and will go
With most coffins. Let us
Quote you; our terms
Are the lowest, and we offer,
Dirt cheap, a place where
It is lovely to lie.

LOYALTIES

The prince walks upon the carpet
Our hearts have unrolled
For him; a worn carpet,
I fear. We are a poor
People; we should have saved up
For this; these rents, these blood stains,
This erosion of the edges
Of it, do him no honour.

And where does it lead to
Anyway? About the table
The shopkeepers are all attention.
I would have run it to the door
Of the holding where Puw lived
Once, wrapping the language
About him, watching the trickle
Of his children down the hill's side.

KNEELING

Moments of great calm,
Kneeling before an altar
Of wood in a stone church
In summer, waiting for the God
To speak; the air a staircase
For silence; the sun's light
Ringing me, as though I acted
A great rôle. And the audiences
Still; all that close throng
Of spirits waiting, as I,
For the message.
           Prompt me, God;
But not yet. When I speak,
Though it be you who speak
Through me, something is lost.
The meaning is in the waiting.

TENANCIES

This is pain's landscape.
A savage agriculture is practised
Here; every farm has its
Grandfather or grandmother, gnarled hands
On the cheque-book, a long, slow
Pull on the placenta about the neck.
Old lips monopolise the talk
When a friend calls. The children listen
From the kitchen; the children march
With angry patience against the dawn.
They are waiting for someone to die
Whose name is as bitter as the soil
They handle. In clear pools
In the furrows they watch themselves grow old
To the terrible accompaniment of the song
Of the blackbird, that promises them love.

NO, SEÑOR

We were out in the hard country.
The railroads kept crossing our path,
Signed with important names,
Salamanca to Madrid,
Malaga to Barcelona.
Sometimes an express went by,
Tubular in the newest fashion;
The faces were a blurred frieze,
A hundred or so city people
Digesting their latest meal,
Over coffee, over a cigarette,
Discussing the news from Viet Nam,
Fondling imaginary wounds
Of the last war, honouring themselves
In the country to which they belonged
By proxy. Their landscape slipped by
On a spool. We saw the asses
Hobbling upon the road
To the village, no Don Quixote
Upon their backs, but all the burden
Of a poor land, the weeds and grasses
Of the mesa. The men walked
Beside them; there was no sound
But the hoarse music of the bells.

COTO DOÑANA

I don't know; ask the place.
It was there when we found it:
Sand mostly, and bushes, too;
Some of them with dry flowers.
The map indicates a lake;
We thought we saw it from the top
Of a sand-dune, but walking brought it
No nearer.
        There are great birds
There that stain the sand
With their shadows, and snakes coil
Their necklaces about the bones
Of the carrion. At night the wild
Boars plough by their tusks'
Moonlight, and fierce insects
Sing, drilling for the blood
Of the humans, whom time's sea
Has left there to ride and dream.

LOOK

Look, here are two cronies, let's
Listen to them as the wind
Creeps under their clothes and the rain
Mixes with the bright moisture
Of their noses. They are saying,
Each in his own way, 'I am dying
And want to live. I am alive
And wish to die'. And for the same
Reason, that they have no belief
In a God who made the world
For misery and for the streams of pain
To flow in. Mildew and pus and decay
They deal in, and feed on mucous
And wind, diet of a wet land. So
They fester and, met now by this tree,
Complain, voices of the earth, talking,
Not as we wanted it to talk,
Who have been reared on its reflections
In art or had its behaviour
Seen to. We must dip belief
Not in dew nor in the cool fountain
Of beech buds, but in seas
Of manure through which they squelch
To the bleakness of their assignations.

ART HISTORY

They made the grey stone
Blossom, setting it on a branch
Of the mind; airy cathedrals
Grew, trembling at the tip
Of their breathing; delicate palaces
Hung motionless in the gold,
Unbelievable sunrise. They praised
With rapt forms such as the blind hand
Dreamed, journeying to its sad
Nuptials. We come too late
On the scene, pelted with the stone
Flowers' bitter confetti.

THE SMALL WINDOW

In Wales there are jewels
To gather, but with the eye
Only. A hill lights up
Suddenly; a field trembles
With colour and goes out
In its turn; in one day
You can witness the extent
Of the spectrum and grow rich

With looking. Have a care;
This wealth is for the few
And chosen. Those who crowd
A small window dirty it
With their breathing, though sublime
And inexhaustible the view.

THEY

I take their hands,
Hard hands. There is no love
For such, only a willed
Gentleness. Negligible men
From the village, from the small
Holdings, they bring their grief
Sullenly to my back door,
And are speechless. Seeing them
In the wind with the light's
Halo, watching their eyes
Blur, I know the reason
They cry, their worsting
By one whom they will fight.

Daily the sky mirrors
The water, the water the
Sky. Daily I take their side
In their quarrel, calling their faults
Mine. How do I serve so
This being they have shut out
Of their houses, their thoughts, their lives?

PLEASE

What do you want of me?
I am here and answer
To my name. I rise, work,
And keep my lusts
To myself. Through tattered sunlight
I go, and make your dreams
Mine. You catch me sobbing
And smile. You curl your lips
At my pleasure, wintering me
For a song, because it was not
Yours; because my pockets
Were empty, and I could sing.

I do not fight
You; it is you who fight
Me, wounding yourself
With blows that I will not give.

AGAIN

What to do? It's the old boredom
Come again: indolent grass,
Wind creasing the water
Hardly at all; a bird floating
Round and round. For one hour
I have known Eden, the still place
We hunger for. My hand lay
Innocent; the mind was idle.

Nothing has changed; the day goes on
With its business, watching itself
In a calm mirror. Yet I know now
I am ready for the sly tone
Of the serpent, ready to climb
My branches after the same fruit.

BURGOS

Nightingales crackled in the frost
At Burgos. The day dawned fiercely
On the parched land, on the fields to the east
Of the city, bitter with sage
And thistle. Lonely bells called
From the villages; no one answered
Them but the sad priests, fingering
Their beads, praying for the lost people
Of the soil. Everywhere were the slow
Donkeys, carrying silent men
To the mesa to reap their bundles
Of dried grass. In the air an eagle
Circled, shadowless as the God
Who made that country and drinks its blood.

STUDY

The flies walk upon the roof top.
The student's eyes are too keen
To miss them. The young girls walk
In the roadway; the wind ruffles
Their skirts. The student does not look.
He sees only the flies spread their wings
And take off into the sunlight
Without sound. There is nothing to do
Now but read in his book
Of how young girls walked in the roadway
In Tyre, and how young men
Sailed off into the red west
For gold, writing dry words
To the music the girls sang.

THAT

It will always win.
Other men will come as I have
To stand here and beat upon it
As on a door, and ask for love,
For compassion, for hatred even; for anything
Rather than this blank indifference,
Than the neutrality of its answers, if they can be called,
    answers
These grey skies, these wet fields,
With the wind's winding-sheet upon them.

And endlessly the days go on
With their business. Lovers make their appearance
And vanish. The germ finds its way
From the grass to the snail to the liver to the grass.
The shadow of the tree falls
On our acres like a crucifixion,
With a bird singing in the branches
What its shrill species has always sung,
Hammering its notes home
One by one into our brief flesh.

THE PLACE

Summer is here.
Once more the house has its
Spray of martins, Proust's fountain
Of small birds, whose light shadows
Come and go in the sunshine
Of the lawn as thoughts do
In the mind. Watching them fly
Is my business, not as a man vowed
To science, who counts their returns
To the rafters, or sifts their droppings
For facts, recording the wave-length
Of their screaming; my method is so
To have them about myself
Through the hours of this brief
Season and to fill with their
Movement, that it is I they build
In and bring up their young
To return to after the bitter
Migrations, knowing the site
Inviolate through its outward changes.